Real Repertoire

for VIOLIN

Selected and edited by Mary Cohen

VIOLIN PART

Contents

Faber Music 3 Queen Square London WC1N 3AU

in association with

Trinity College London 89 Albert Embankment London SE1 7TP

ALLEGRO

from Sonata in D minor

Jean-Baptiste Senaillé
(1687–1730)

ALLEGRO AND MENUETTO

from Serenade No.2

Wolfgang Amadeus Mozart
(1756–1791)

CHANSON TRISTE
Op.40 No.2

Pyotr Ilyich Tchaikovsky
(1840–1893)

LARGHETTO

from Sonatina Op.100

Antonín Dvořák
(1841–1904)

* Optional: top notes only

SALUT D'AMOUR

Edward Elgar
(1857–1934)

To make this accessible to players, some of the fingering has been simplified, whilst retaining as much of Elgar's intended style as possible.

ALLEGRO MOLTO

from Sonata in D major

Franz Schubert
(1797–1828)

AN EVENING IN THE VILLAGE

Béla Bartók
(1881–1945)

HUNGARIAN DANCE

No.5

Johannes Brahms
(1831–1897)

CHANSON POLONAISE
Op.12

Henryk Wieniawski
(1835–1880)

LARGO AND ALLEGRO

from Sonata in F major Op.1 No.12

(*attrib.*) George Frideric Handel
(1685–1759)

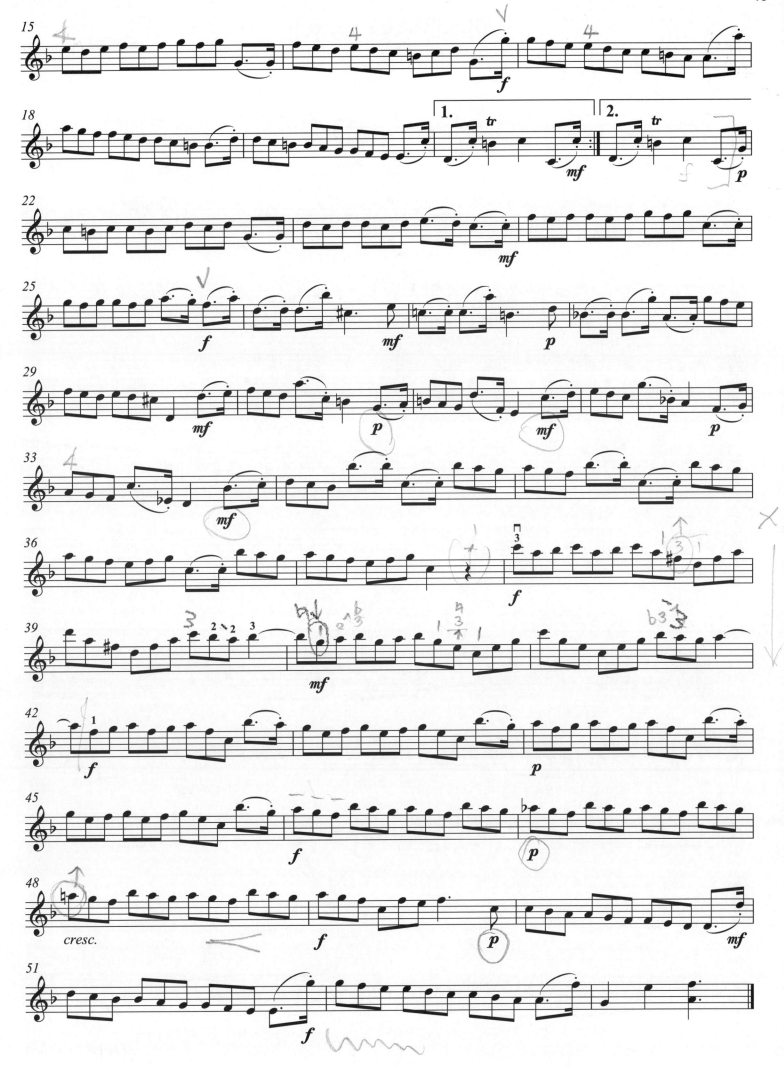

BOURRÉES I and II

from Suite No.3

Johann Sebastian Bach
(1685–1750)
(*unaccompanied*)

Bourrée I da capo

TRINITY REPERTOIRE LIBRARY

for VIOLIN

Selected and edited by Mary Cohen

PIANO ACCOMPANIMENT

Contents

Faber Music 3 Queen Square London WC1N 3AU
in association with
Trinity College London 89 Albert Embankment London SE1 7TP

EDITOR'S NOTE

Real Repertoire for Violin is suitable for intermediate players, providing a wide choice of enjoyable music for study and performance. The music ranges from the Baroque period to the 20th century and can be combined to make interesting programmes for festivals, concerts or examinations.

I have prepared these pieces as playing editions to give a helpful introduction to the repertoire for the grade 4–6 player. The fingering and bowing have been chosen with great care to produce good technical and musical results that are achievable by players of this standard. Metronome marks have been provided as a guide but are not obligatory and in the pieces from the earlier periods expression marks have been suggested. To assist the less experienced player some simpler options have also been included. I do recommend that at a future stage players should start to develop their own ideas regarding fingering, bowing, dynamics and so on.

I hope these pieces will bring as much pleasure to you as they have to myself and my pupils!

Mary Cohen

© 2003 by Faber Music Ltd and Trinity College *London*
First published in 2003 by Faber Music Ltd
in association with Trinity College *London*
3 Queen Square London WC1N 3AU
Cover design by Nick Flower
Music processed by Jackie Leigh
Printed in England by Caligraving Ltd

ISBN 0-571-52155-X

To buy Faber Music or Trinity publications or to find out about the full range of titles available please contact your local music retailer or Faber Music sales enquiries:

Faber Music Ltd, Burnt Mill, Elizabeth Way, Harlow CM20 2HX
Tel: +44 (0)1279 82 89 82   Fax: +44 (0)1279 82 89 83
sales@fabermusic.com   fabermusic.com   trinitycollege.co.uk

ALLEGRO

from Sonata in D minor

Jean-Baptiste Senaillé
(1687–1730)

ALLEGRO AND MENUETTO

from Serenade No.2

Wolfgang Amadeus Mozart
(1756–1791)

Menuetto

♩ = c.132

Menuetto da capo

CHANSON TRISTE
Op.40 No.2

Pyotr Ilyich Tchaikovsky
(1840–1893)

LARGHETTO
from Sonatina Op.100

Antonín Dvořák
(1841–1904)

* Optional: top notes only

* Optional: top notes only

SALUT D'AMOUR

Edward Elgar
(1857–1934)

To make this accessible to players, some of the fingering has been simplified, whilst retaining as much of Elgar's intended style as possible.

ALLEGRO MOLTO
from Sonata in D major

Franz Schubert
(1797–1828)

24

26

AN EVENING IN THE VILLAGE

Béla Bartók
(1881–1945)

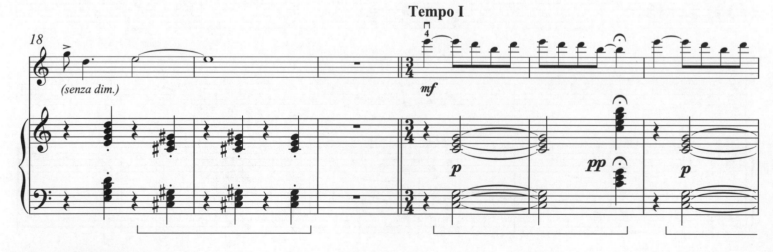

HUNGARIAN DANCE
No.5

Johannes Brahms
(1831–1897)

CHANSON POLONAISE
Op.12

Henryk Wieniawski
(1835–1880)

LARGO AND ALLEGRO

from Sonata in F major Op.1 No.12

(*attrib.*) George Frideric Handel
(1685–1759)